I0814615

Intro to Portuguese

Bela Davis

Português

Abdo Kids Junior
is an Imprint of Abdo Kids
abdobooks.com

Abdo
INTRO TO LANGUAGE
Kids

abdobooks.com

Published by Abdo Kids, a division of ABDO, P.O. Box 398166, Minneapolis, Minnesota 55439.

Printed in the United States of America, North Mankato, Minnesota.

102024

012025

Consultant: Ursula Decker Ramalho

Photo Credits: Getty Images, Shutterstock

Production Contributors: Teddy Borth, Jennie Forsberg, Grace Hansen

Design Contributors: Candice Keimig, Colleen McLaren

Library of Congress Control Number: 2024936629

Publisher's Cataloging-in-Publication Data

Names: Davis, Bela, author.

Title: Intro to Portuguese / by Bela Davis

Description: Minneapolis, Minnesota : Abdo Kids, 2025 | Series: Intro to language set 2 | Includes online resources and index.

Identifiers: ISBN 9798384902850 (lib. bdg.) | ISBN 9798384903550 (ebook) | ISBN 9798384903901 (Read-to-me ebook)

Subjects: LCSH: Informal language learning--Juvenile literature. | Language and languages--Juvenile literature. | Bilingual books--Juvenile literature. | Language acquisition--Juvenile literature.

Classification: DDC 418--dc23

Table of Contents

Intro to Portuguese

Portuguese is spoken around the world. Let's learn some words!

Portuguese	**bem-vindo**
(sound guide)	(behm-veen•doh)
English	**welcome**

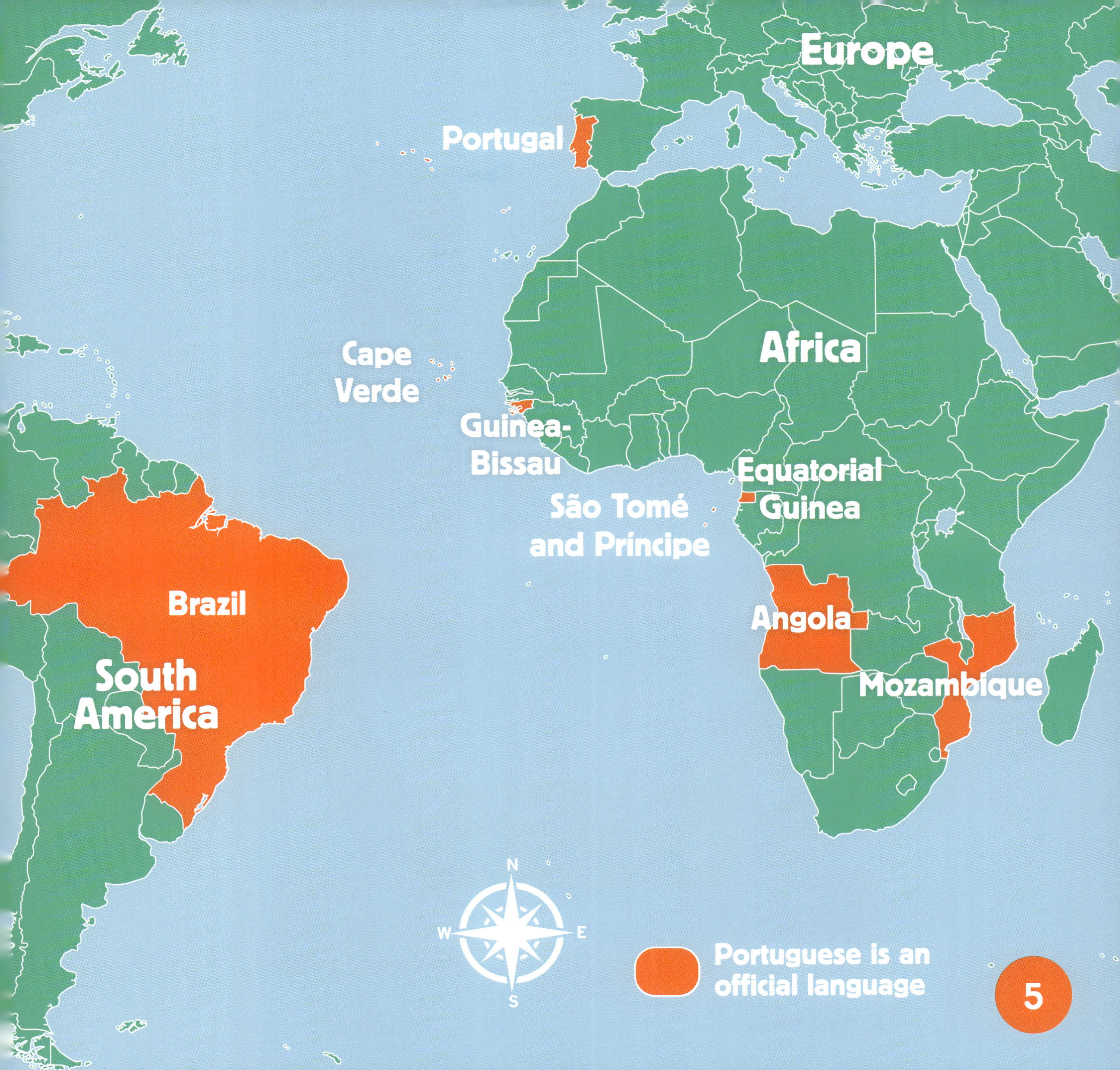
Europe
Portugal
Africa
Cape Verde
Guinea-Bissau
Equatorial Guinea
São Tomé and Príncipe
Brazil
South America
Angola
Mozambique
N
W
E
S
Portuguese is an official language

used with masculine nouns
used with feminine nouns
(m) um/uma (f)
(oon/oo•mah)
one
(m) dois/duas (f)
(doh•eesh/doo•ahsh)
two
seis
(say•eesh)
six
sete
(seh•chee)
seven

três
(tray•eess)
three

quatro
(kwa•troo)
four

cinco
(sin•koo)
five

oito
(oy•too)
eight

nove
(noh•vee)
nine

dez
(day•iss)
ten

onze
(on•zee)
eleven

doze
(doh•zee)
twelve

dezesseis
(dee•zeh•say•iss)
sixteen

dezessete
(chee•zeh•seh•chee)
seventeen

treze
(tray•zee)
thirteen

catorze
(ka•tor•zee)
fourteen

quinze
(keen•zee)
fifteen

dezoito
(chee•zoy•too)
eighteen

dezenove
(chee•zeh•noh•vee)
nineteen

vinte
(veen•tchee)
twenty

cores
(kohr•eess)
colors
verde
(vehr•deh)
green
amarelo
(ah•mah•reh•loh)
yellow
laranja
(lah•rahn•zhah)
orange
azul
(ah•zool)
blue

vermelho
(vehr•meh•lyo)
red
roxo
(hoh•shoh)
purple
branco
(brahn•koh)
white
preto
(preh•toh)
black

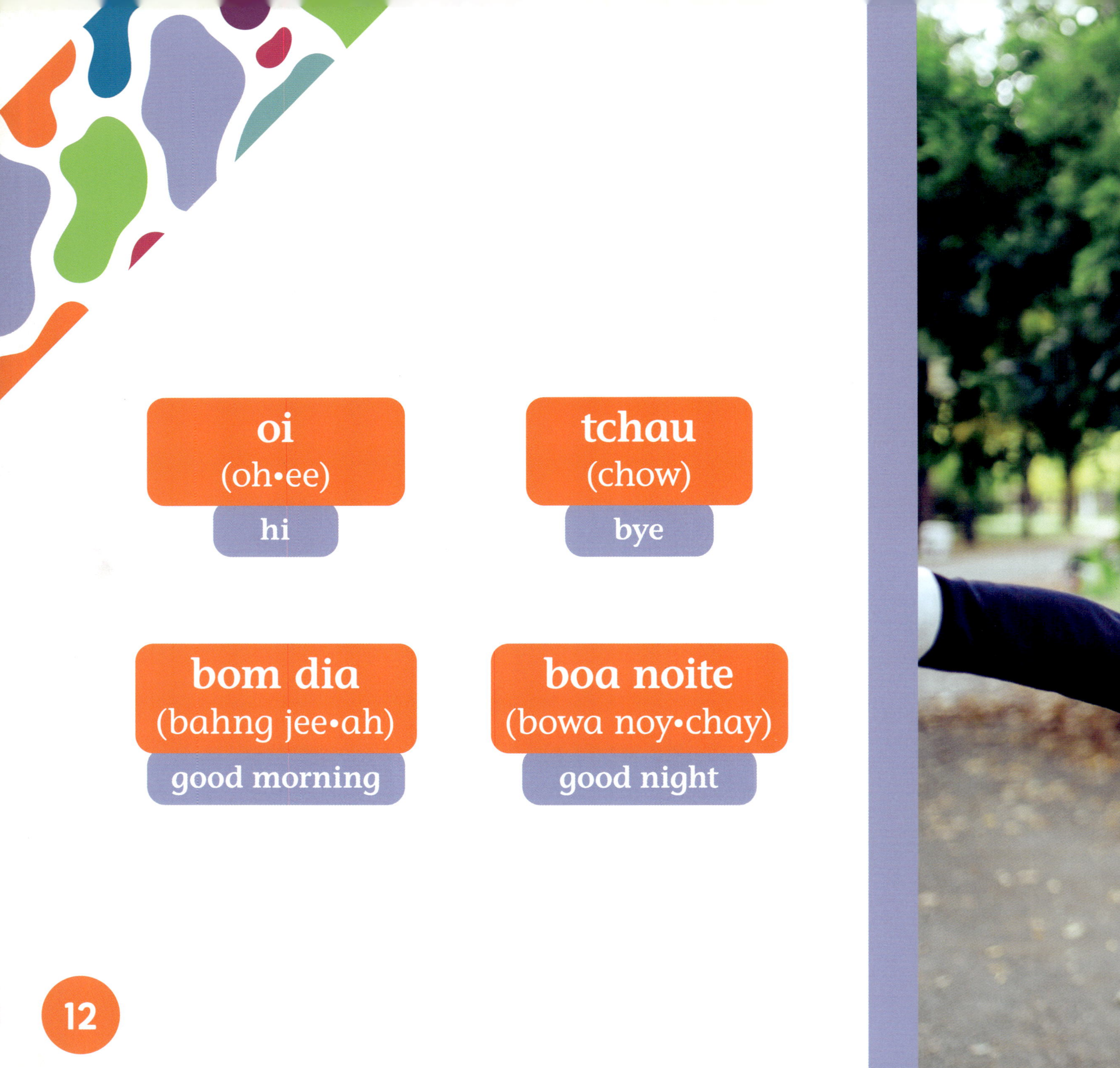

oi
(oh•ee)
hi

tchau
(chow)
bye

bom dia
(bahng jee•ah)
good morning

boa noite
(bowa noy•chay)
good night

por favor
(pohr fa•vohr)
please

obrigado
(oh•bree•gah•doo)
thank you

sim
(seem)
yes

não
(now)
no

família
(fa•mee•lee•ah)
family

mãe
(mai)
mother

pai
(pai)
father

irmã
(eer•ma)
sister

irmão
(eer•maow)
brother

avó
(ah•voh)
grandmother

avô
(ah•vou)
grandfather

tia
(chee•ah)
aunt

tio
(chee•yu)
uncle

animais
(ah•nee•mais)
animals
gato
(gah•too)
male cat
gata
(gah•tah)
female cat

pássaro
(pah•sah•roo)
bird
cachorro
(ka•shohr•roh)
male dog
cadela
(ka•de•la)
female dog
peixe
(peh•shee)
fish

lugares (loo•gah•rees) – Places

casa
(ka•zah)
house

escola
(ees•koh•la)
school

parque
(pahr•kee)
park

praia
(pry•ah)
beach

alfabeto (ahl•fah•bet•toh) – Alphabet

letter / Portuguese pronunciation	A	B	C	D	E
	ah	beh	seh	deh	eh

F	G	H	I	J	K	L
eff	geh	ah•gah	ee	joh•tah	kah	elee

M	N	O	P	Q	R	S
emee	enee	oh	peh	keh	ehee	esee

T	U	V	W	X	Y	Z
te	oo	veh	dah•blee ooh	shees	eep-see-lon	ze

special cases / sounds	CH	NH	LH	RR	Ç
	shh	ny	ly	rolled rr	sss

Index

Visit **abdokids.com** to access crafts, games, videos, and more!

Use Abdo Kids code

IIK2850

or scan this QR code!